To Ronald —
Hope you

I FEEL THE SAME WAY

Lilian Moore

I FEEL THE SAME WAY

LILIAN MOORE

Illustrations by Robert Quackenbush

AN ALADDIN BOOK
Atheneum

To Carl and Micky, the brothers with whom I shared my childhood | L.M.

For all my family, and all my friends, and for the child in me | R.Q.

Wind Poem (Wind Song) AND *Dragon Smoke*
WERE ORIGINALLY PRINTED IN THE
Lucky Book Club Memo to Teachers
COPYRIGHT © 1966 BY SCHOLASTIC MAGAZINES, INC.

TEXT COPYRIGHT © 1967 BY LILLIAN MOORE
ILLUSTRATIONS COPYRIGHT © 1967 BY ROBERT QUACKENBUSH
ALL RIGHTS RESERVED
PUBLISHED SIMULTANEOUSLY IN CANADA BY
MCCLELLAND & STEWART, LTD.
MANUFACTURED IN THE UNITED STATES OF AMERICA BY
CONNECTICUT PRINTERS, INC., HARTFORD
ISBN 0-689-70424-0
FIRST ALADDIN EDITION

WAKING

My secret way of waking
is like a place
to hide.
I'm very still,
my eyes are shut.
They all think I am sleeping
but
I'm wide awake inside.

They all think I am sleeping
but
I'm wiggling my toes.
I feel sun-fingers
on my cheek.
I hear voices whisper-speak.
I squeeze my eyes
to keep them shut
so they will think I'm sleeping
BUT
I'm really wide awake inside
—and no one knows!

IN THE SUN

Sit
on your doorstep
or any place.

Sit
in the sun
and lift your face.

Close your eyes and
sun dream.
Soon the warm warm sun
will seem
to fill you up
and
spill over.

ANTS LIVE HERE

Ants live here
by the curb stone,
see?
They worry a lot
about giants like
me.

HEY, BUG!

Hey, bug, stay!
Don't run away.
I know a game that we can play.

I'll hold my fingers very still
and you can climb a finger-hill.

No, no.
Don't go.

Here's a wall——a tower, too,
a tiny bug town, just for you.
I've a cookie. You have some.
Take this oatmeal cookie crumb.

Hey, bug, stay!
Hey, bug!
Hey!

RAIN RIVERS

It's raining.
Street streams and rain rivers
are flowing,
and little twig boats
are towing
leaf barges.

OUTSIDE

I
am inside
looking outside
at the pelting
rain—
where
the outside world
is melting
upon my
window
pane.

UNTIL I SAW THE SEA

Until I saw the sea
I did not know
that wind
could wrinkle water so.

I never knew
that sun
could splinter a whole sea of blue.

Nor
did I know before,
a sea breathes in and out
upon a shore.

MINE

I made a sand castle.
In rolled the sea.
> "All sand castles
> belong to me—
> to me,"

said the sea.

I dug sand tunnels.
In flowed the sea.
> "All sand tunnels
> belong to me—
> to me,"

said the sea.

I saw my sand pail floating free.
I ran and snatched it from the sea.
> "My sand pail
> belongs to me—
> to ME!"

SOMETIMES

Sometimes
when I skip or hop
or when I'm
      jumping

Suddenly
I like to stop
and listen to me
      thumping.

HOW TO GO AROUND A CORNER

Corners
are
the places
where
streets run down to meet.

Corners
are
surprises
on almost any street.

At
almost
any corner
it's best to wait

and
turn
the corner
slowly
as if it had a gate.

WALKING

I stop—
        it stops, too.
It goes when I do.

Over my shoulder I can see
The moon is taking a walk with me.

IF YOU CATCH A FIREFLY

If you catch a firefly
      and keep it in a jar
You may find that
      you have lost
A tiny star.

If you let it go then,
      back into the night,
You may see it
      once again
Star bright.

GO WIND

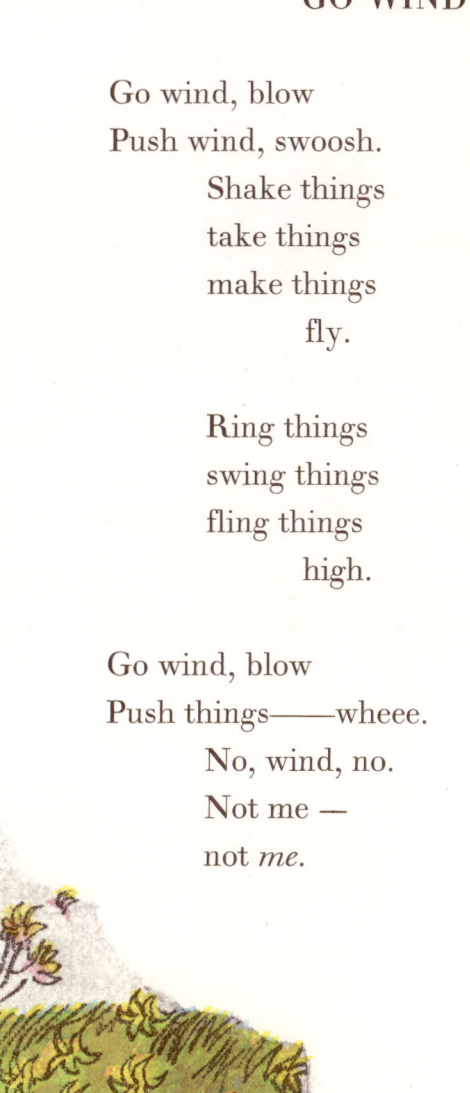

Go wind, blow
Push wind, swoosh.
    Shake things
    take things
    make things
        fly.

    Ring things
    swing things
    fling things
        high.

Go wind, blow
Push things——wheee.
    No, wind, no.
    Not me —
    not *me*.

WIND SONG

When the wind blows
The quiet things speak.
Some whisper, some clang,
Some creak.

Grasses swish.
Treetops sigh.
Flags slap
and snap at the sky.
Wires on poles
whistle and hum.
Ashcans roll.
Windows drum.

When the wind goes—
suddenly
then,
the quiet things
are quiet again.

RED

All day
across the way
on someone's sill
a geranium glows
red bright
like a
tiny
faraway
traffic light.

TRUE

When
the green eyes
of a cat
look deep into
you

you know
that
whatever it is
they are saying
is
true.

DRAGON SMOKE

Breathe and blow
white clouds
    with every puff.
It's cold today,
    cold enough
to see your breath.
Huff!
    Breathe dragon smoke
      today!

FOG

Did the spiders
      come out last night to
      play?
Did they spin and spin
      the night
      away?
Is that why the world
      is cobweb gray
      today?

IN THE FOG

Stand still.
The fog wraps you up
and no one can find you.

Walk.
The fog opens up
to let you through
and closes behind you.

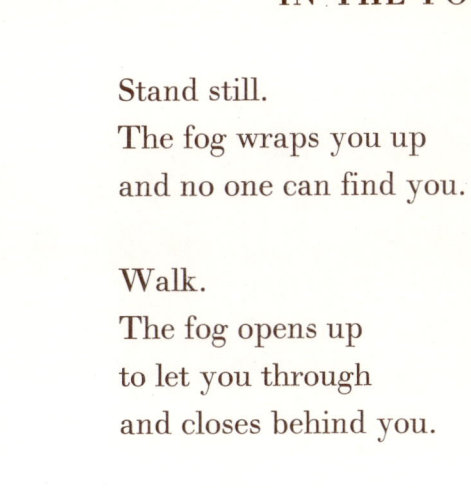

TWILIGHT

The sky is bright
with left-over day.
The night is not quite
here.
In the no-longer light
and not-yet dark
all things are shadow-clear.